UNDER THE WINGS

UNDER THE WINGS

Stephen Scriver

Coteau Books

All poems © Stephen Scriver, 1991.

All rights reserved. No part of this book covered by the copyrights hereon may be reproduced or used in any form or by any means—graphic, electronic or mechanical—without the prior written permission of the publisher. Any request for photocopying, recording, taping or information storage and retrieval systems of any part of this book shall be directed in writing to the Canadian Reprography Collective, 379 Adelaide Street West, Suite M1, Toronto, Ontario M5V 1S5.

Edited by Dennis Cooley.

Cover and book design by Shelley Sopher.

Historic cover photograph courtesy of Maurice Winton. Newspaper courtesy of *The Leader-Post* and the Saskatchewan Archives Board. All interior photographs courtesy of the Scriver family, except page vi and vii courtesy of Maurice Winton.

Typeset by Lines and Letters.

Printed and bound in Canada by Hignell Printing Ltd.

The publisher gratefully acknowledges the financial assistance of the Saskatchewan Arts Board, the Canada Council and the Department of Communications.

The author would like to thank Roman Waldbillig, Harold Baller, Ed Brunanski, Bob Whatley, and the late Walter Baller who told him the stories, who are part of the story. And thanks to his late Dad, Harry Scriver, a storyteller who started it all.

Canadian Cataloguing in Publication Data

Scriver, Stephen, 1947-

    Under the wings

    Poems.
    ISBN 1-55050-016-3

1. Canada. Royal Canadian Air Force – Poetry. 2. World War, 1939-1945 – Canada – Poetry. I. Title.

PS8587.C75U6 1991   C811/.54   C91-097022-X
PR9199.3.S375U6 1991

COTEAU BOOKS
401– 2206 Dewdney Avenue
Regina, Saskatchewan
Canada
S4R 1H3

to Mom, Barb and Linda and women who wait

RCAF Lancaster Bomber, 426 Squadron

THE ORIGIN OF THE WORD "ERK"

erg—the lowest unit of work
erk—short for "aircraftsman" as in the song "One of the Aircs"
erk—a pimp
erk—as in "irk" e.g. "They irk me, these erks!"

THE ERKS MOTTO

Illegitamus non Carborundum

(Don't let the bastards grind you down.)

so me an Hall just wandered
through the streets
of Halifax   tryin to hide
the shit on our boots   thinkin
about all that water   an U-boat
stories we heard in bars
the Jerries pickin off survivors
like ducks on a pond

an I don't know why
but for the trip across
we bought some summer sausage
an OXO cubes   in case
we got torpedoed

well   it turned out
when we boarded   here we were
five thousand troops   stuffed in
this holiday liner built for
two thousand   an the mess hall
smelled so bad   if the sea
didn't make you sick   the stench
down there sure as hell would

but we're like kings   me an Hall
sittin on our stash   an somehow
we'd kipe a loaf of bread
to make it interesting

an jeez   all around us
guys were sick as dogs   this one fella
lyin there moanin   "Lemme die, guys,
come on, forget it, lemme die"
but once in a while we'd get
some OXO an water down his throat
an still today he claims
we saved his life   when we see him
at reunions

well   we got over after all
none the worse for wear
an the only bad thing was me an Hall
were the only guys probably well enough
to stand on deck all day
gawkin across that pukey gray swamp
for swastika flags
an periscopes

one more thing
about that ride across the pond

lookin over that endless swamp
reminded me of doin summerfallow
the endless rounds   endless boredom
that finally got me over to Hall's
forty acres   an we cooked up this
volunteerin for the air force scheme

an boy
when that ship started feelin
like our old Massey tractor
I stood on that deck
an damn near cried

I smoked for over forty years
regretted every last puff

but see
soon as we got overseas
there wasn't much goin on
so we got stuck diggin trenches

the first day   about ten
the Sarge   he comes along an bellers
"OK boys! Smoke break!"
so I take a breather

well
the Sarge   he looks at me
like I just pissed on his ribbons
an he sez   "What the hell you doin?"

". . . don't smoke, Sarge" I sez

"So lean into that stinkin shovel, boy!"

well
you don't have to hit me
with no ballpeen hammer
next day you know who
's got a pack of fags

I remember after bein there a week
we were still wonderin where the hell
this war was

        till one day
this Blenheim twin-engine job
comes limpin into our base
back from a daylight raid

we can see she's all shot up
so we run out for a closer look

well
I run around the front   an stop
dead in my tracks   cause I'm lookin
at what used to be the navigator's bubble
an there he sits   what's left of him
anyways   still strapped in   unconscious
maybe dead   legs half shot away   blood
caked from his knees to his chest

so I don't know how long
I stand there   gawkin
till someone shoves me outa the way

you know
I didn't eat for two days
an weeks after that I wasn't sure
if I'd ever see my goddamn home
or family again

talk about just off the farm

our first base was Topcliffe
an when we got there
an M.O. got us in a lecture hall
an told us that this base
was the worst
for V.D.

well
once someone explained to me
what V.D. was
I was scared shitless   that is
until someone else explained
how you got it

at least we had somethin to do
day in   day out
but it musta bin the shits
for the army guys
waitin years (before I got there even)
for somethin to happen

not knowin if they were
just on maneuvers again   or
if the next time was the invasion
we heard about month after month
in the pubs

but they caused a lot of crap too
sittin around so long   like
whole towns ripped apart
stores looted   women attacked
I guess they'd just go nuts

but you wanna know
my theory is
that's what Dieppe was all about
cause after the guys in Britain
saw the films of what happened
to the South Saskatchewan boys
they got a little better
at waitin

oh yeah
we even had a few Yankees
volunteerin early on

guess I remember old Omaha the best
yeah Omaha   cause that's where he was from

just a kid lookin for a thrill
an he'd been turned down in the States
cause of his asthma

so this one night Omaha he's pulled
the graveyard shift on guard duty
over by the ammo dump
an damned if there isn't a raid

so Jerry's droppin these chandalier flares
lightin the place up like
high noon at Piccadilly
an before you know it
here comes Omaha racin across the tarmac
a 109 Messerschmitt tryin to drill
a matchin arsehole in his backside

well
once things settle down
Omaha shows us a shell hole
through his pants   about three inches
below the family jewels

an I never told anyone to this day
but about a week later
I find him in the hut
poundin his mattress
inhalin the dust
so's he can get his asthma goin

so it's not a fortnight
before Omaha's got his bags packed
his discharge from the M.O.
in his hand   an those chandalier flares
still flashin in his eyes

okay
this one day we're sittin around
the orderly room   right
an in comes Warrant Officer Smythe
a big grin on his face   this letter
in his hand an he sez "Hey fellas!
Listen to this one!"

an he reads:

"Dear Sir,

I am inquiring about an LAC Green
who I believe is a mechanic
in your squadron. I have known
LAC Green for the period
of three months   during which time
he had made both my daughter an myself
pregnant. This situation
we can cope with quite well,
but would you please have him
return a bicycle he borrowed
on his last visit to our home."

well
we gotta see this guy
so when the laughin settles down
the W.O. dispatches a runner
to bring in Green
who's an air framer
out on the dispersals

jeez
we damn near tear our baggage
when in comes this little
greasy runt   about five foot one

the W.O. he puts him at ease
askin him if he's workin hard
an how he feels today an
does he happen to know this Mrs.
So-an-so   an did he happen
to borrow her bicycle

Green sez he does an he did
an he'll return it   soon
as he's got a pass

about a week later
in he comes an reports
the bike's back home

Smythe asks him how the Mrs.
an her daughter are feelin
an Green sez they're not so bad
an he'll be seein them again soon

well
D day it ain't
but it's the best war story
I got

we had a few Ojibways from North Ontario
in our outfit   they weren't much
as airmen an mostly got put
on work details an joe jobs

but Lord sonny Jesus
did the British women ever like them

guess those birds had seen
one too many dusters
at the flicks   some musta
had ideas about totem poles
pintos an that kinda stuff

what I heard was
a couple of them even got hitched
an actually got to Canada
but boy when they saw
the reservation   bam   they were back
across the pond
before their tea got cold

oh yeah
then there's this one time
we just arrived at this one base
an this la-de-da Pongo sergeant
is showin us around

an see
on the front of a kite's wings
there's these Vs cut out
an each one's fitted
with this spring-loaded blade
that snaps out an cuts up
all the wire an junk
the Jerries threw up with their flak

so this Pongo's gonna explain
to us colonials
these things we've seen
a hundred times before
an in his explanation
he demonstrates by snappin
his finger in one of these Vs

an goddamned if this goddamned blade
don't snap off his goddamned finger

like think of it
we're standin there   stunned
not knowin whether to laugh cry
shit or go blind
cause it seems like the whole thing
is part of his demo

an there he stands
gawkin at this stump
squirtin blood down his dress blues
like a pig's neck at killin time

by God
it must've bin some sight
for those nurses   six gigglin Canucks
luggin in that fainted Pongo

sure
a lotta guys brought back
good women after the war
but there were a few more
who got taken for a ride

you see
if a woman married a serviceman
she got thirty-five bucks a month
plus half his pay   say
about twenty bucks more
damn good for those times

an if he got killed
she was set for life
with a widow's pension

like
I remember this one time
a guy comes into the orderly room
an fills out what we called
an A.P.M.—you know, Application
for Permission to Marry

well
it gets passed through to the W.O.
an about half an hour later
in comes this second guy
an he fills out an A.P.M. too

so
this guy is halfway out the door
when the W.O. comes out yellin
"Jimmy   hey Jimmy   Get back here!"

the kid turns at the door
an the W.O. throws the form
right in his face   sayin
"Sorry Jimmy   it's no good!"

"Why not, eh? Did I fill it out wrong
or somethin?"

"No, kid, but you're about a half hour late.
Some other guy's got her already!"

ya
the world's moved pretty fast
since then   an even though
I've done okay   the one thing
I miss more'n anything
is the guys

you see   me an Hall somehow
got posted to different bases
an here I was   a couple
hundred guys just thrown together
an we just had to get along

but as the war went on
we developed this kind of
feeling you know
for one another

well face it
we ate an slept an worked
side by side   went to the pubs
drank a few pails of beer
fought a few Yanks   chased the birds

an no one ever asked you
if you were a lawyer or
a farmer's son or if you
were French or English
or what church you went to

an specially us erks
you know   the muckers
we had more of that feelin
than the others   cause we knew
we were around for the duration

ya
those were real pals
you know   true blue buddies
an somehow   I just never
had that feelin again

I never did take
to the Brits too much
especially the officers
we'd get sometimes

you'd go to meals   an there
they'd be sittin by themselves
an one thing I remember
was the way they wouldn't
take the top slice of bread
from the pile   always
lifted it up an took the next one
guess they never
went through the thirties

but I guess
the thing that bugged me
the most was the way
they'd look over at us
an then say somethin like
"Think the rain'll hurt the potatoes?"
an one of the others would say
"Might hurt the little ones"

made you wonder
what the hell you were doin
fightin to keep the krauts
off their island

the Swede was our good luck charm

like
he was only the mid-upper gunner
but any kite he went up in
came back   three engines
sometimes two   spittin smoke
fuselage lookin like Maggie's drawers
the Swede always brought them back

hell
get this
one time he changes kites
for one mission   an damned
if his last crew
doesn't go down   ka-fuckin-boom
over France   on their next operation

an he kept signin on
for more tours too   till
he finally got in over a hundred
missions   like   ten lifetimes
for most air crew

he never seemed too bright   the Swede
never said more'n three words
in a row   but sure as Hitler had crabs
the Swede had luck

this one time
the Swede's kite comes back
from a raid   full of holes
whistlin like a Stuka
us erks are waitin
for her to disintegrate
but she touches down   makes it
somehow   in one piece

we rush out there   the Swede's
in his bubble   pointin
at these shell holes
on either side   so we go up
an stick this rod through
them   with the Swede still inside

well
the only way we can get
this rod through
is with the Swede pushed
so far up or back
he can't hardly breathe

when he hits the tarmac
we're laughin like arseholes
an the Swede says somethin
like "Don't recall even
duckin, guys" just before
he spills his supper
all over our shoes

you shoulda seen the looker
the Swede brought home
tall   blonde   built
like Betty Grable   legs?
Jesus Murphy   legs
could make a priest cry
an the face of an angel

an talk?   Baby   Baby
she hardly stopped to breathe
which was okay   cause the Swede
(like I said)   didn't say much
anyways

an I don't care what anyone says
she was no tart
come from a good English family
an took to the Swede
like fire to kerosene

well
we married them off
in this big church in Brighton
I was an usher   in fact
all the Swede's ground crew
got an invite

last I heard
they were in Toronto   the two
of them   the Swede some executive
in some big outfit   an the blonde
raisin seven kids   all big Swedes
an built blondes

an I guess
you could say the Swede
's luck is still runnin good

between the runways
were these patches of asphalt
we called the dispersals   each one
with three kites   gettin ready
for the next raid

well
that's where I wanted to be
out in the fresh air
rain shine or snow
I didn't give a shit   just somewhere
away from the brass

you see
this was before they put
all us Canucks together
in Number Six Bomber Group
an here I was   stuck
in the hangers with these
tight-assed Pongo officers

so every morning here we'd be
standin on the parade square
for inspection   these Pongos
dressin us down for bein
what they called "colonial slobs"
an I'd just read my paper
ignorin them

hell   I was always in crap
up to my arse   scuffed shoes
shirt hangin out   forgettin to salute
mostly what they called
insubordination

damned if I didn't
spend four of my first six months
in Britain   C.B.ed

so then I pulled a fast one
on those s.o.b.s
cause they threatened to put me
out on the dispersals
if I didn't smarten up

well
you never saw a sorrier sight
than me   dirty uniform
unshaved   an sure enough
one day they're givin me a hard time
sendin me on their joe jobs
so I says to this corporal
"Why don't you stick a broom
up my arse   an I could sweep
the place up while I'm at it!"

so that's it
the snivelin bastards banish me
to the dispersals

an you know
I could tell things were goin my way
cause I'm walkin out there
like the rabbit in the briar patch
I looks down an right there
on the tarmac is this shilling note

an jeez
I'da summerfallowed the whole stinkin base
with a smile on my face
that day

I guess
we got mostly mutton
an I don't mean lamb neither
no sirree   just plain old mutton
that smelled like someone
put his dirty skivvies in the oven
but it tasted worse

an if that wasn't bad enough
they used the fat to boil
the left-over spuds in
so everything tasted
pretty much the same

then for some variety
they'd give us fish
an that was mostly rotten too
so every once in a while
we'd just turn our plates over
on the tables an walk out

then the officers
would have to come an talk to us
sayin things were gonna improve

which they did for a week or so
cause we probably got a bit
of the officer's grub

but then it's back
to the same old crap
all over again

we'd always finish supper
in about ten minutes
but for a while there
they'd make us sit around
the mess hall for half an hour

so we'd have a smoke
tryin to get an argument goin
so's maybe there'd be a fight
outside later on

this one day the menu board
says we're eatin rabbit stew
but some of us
who'd gone through
the thirties on the farm
figger it's more like horse

well
we're goin pretty good
on that one   till finally
the head cook comes by
to see what the hell's goin on

I sez "Hey, sergeant
what was that stuff really—
rabbit or horse?"

he sez   "Well, sonny boy,
actually it was half an half—
one rabbit an one horse!"

pretty soon
they started bringin in
these Jerry P.O.W.s
to do the dirty work
us erks were usually stuck with

so we'd be headin for the pubs
an they'd look over
from their diggin trenches
or escortin trash

an boy
they were a ratty-lookin bunch
standin by the fence   hand out
yellin "Cee-ga-ret, Jo-nee, cee-ga-ret!"

an if the guards didn't mind
we'd usually toss one over

so
they'd pick it up
look you right in the eye
smile an say somethin
in kraut

well
I don't know no kraut
but I could tell
they weren't sayin
"Thanks a lot, pal!"

they'd usually give us leeway
gettin back from leaves
an I never really pushed my luck
but wouldn't you know it
sure as shit   the first time
I'm an hour late   some bugger
turns me in   an I'm on report

so every day I have to show up
like some school kid
all spit an polished
at eight, noon, an six
then off to K.P.

the first two days
was scrubbin pots an pans
till my hands start to bleed
so I get switched to the spud peeler
this rotatin pail lined with bakelite
that scrapes off the peel
an leaves you the eyes to dig out

well
I get this idea
the more peel you scrape off
the less eyes you gotta dig
so I leave the spuds in longer
till they're just the size
of gopher nuts   an goddamned if
I don't get two more days C.B.
when the Sarge sees this

that's when they put me
on the hash line   an here I stand
this ladle in my hand
servin lemon jello to 800 guys
from this big vat   an all
I remember is diggin down
800 times   till the sweat
was pourin off my face
down my arms an
into that yellow jello
like starin at the sun

they said that Yorkshire
was the pisspot of England—
the clouds would just circle
till they found it
an then let'er go

but rain wasn't the only thing
it attracted   cause Number Six
Bomber Group was the biggest target
around   so we'd get raided
once or twice a week

an there we'd be
hidin in the trees
letters from home stuffed
in our P.J.s   screamin
"Come on, you dumb bastards!
Can't you hit nothin! Take out
our hut once an for all!"

but I'll tell you
if we did as little damage
to them as they did to us
we'da been better off
droppin rocks from carrier pigeons

a lot of our reject kites
like the Sterlings an Wimpies
were sent over to flight school
which was unfortunate
cause these flyin coffins
probably killed as many crews
as Jerry did

anyways
this one time
I get assigned to guard duty
over this pranged Sterling
in some farmer's field
after the bodies were dragged away
thank God

well
it's pretty boring work
so I wander around
till I trip into this
sort of depression

an I nearly crap
when it dawns on me
that this is the last thing left
of some poor kid
who slept through the lecture
about not bein able
to open your chute
a hundred yards above the ground

one Sunday mornin
we're in this hanger
puttin de-icer on these Wimpies
an we bitch enough
that the Sarge lets us go
for a coffee break

we're just sittin down
when we hear this rat-a-tat-tat
as a couple of Jerry fighters
strafe the base

while we're under the tables
they make a couple passes
hit every one of the Wimpies
we're workin on
an kill three guys
sleepin off hangovers
in the huts

makes you wonder eh?

only a couple weeks
after that raid   I'm gettin
ready for a three-day leave
an about bloody time too

so I pull my dress blues
down from the shelf
above my bunk

well
I don't know
whether to laugh or cry
when I find these Jerry shell holes
through every single piece

if you had a brother
in the same service as you
you could put what they called
a "claim" on him
so's he could be transferred
to the same base

well
this one fella puts in a claim
on his little brother
an is happier than a screwed sailor
when the kid arrives

a week later
the kid's on flight duty
walks straight into a propeller

you know
I got one shot in overseas
no shit   it was like this

you see
this one night Flight Sergeant Jones
gets me   Slim   an Ernie
out of our bunks   an has
that shit-eatin grin of his

he sez
"Hey farm boys, we're goin huntin'!"

so
he issues us with these Lee Enfields
like we used back home
for shootin deer   an for a minute
I'm thinkin   this Christly guy
is on the level

well Jonesy   he
explains that some kraut P.O.W.s
've taken off   an someone's seen them
around these abandoned Dakotas
out past the dispersals

we go down there
an can hear them fiddlin around
inside one of these kites
i guess figgerin they're gonna get
back to the Fatherland in

Jonesy tells me to fire
a round through the fuselage
so I let'er have it

boy
they don't look like no Master Race
when they come slinkin
outa there like gophers who
just seen a weasel down their hole

so after we hustled them
back to their compound   you could say
my war was over   cause we turned
in those rifles
an went back to bed

for a while
we had this preacher's kid
in our hut   (nicknamed P.K.
of course)   an he's lily-white
always lookin at us
sideways   when we swore
or farted or talked
about women an drinkin

but one time
old P.K.'s out on the coal pile
fillin the pail for the night
an in comes this 109

well
it makes a quick pass
an tries to plug our boy

P.K. he comes barrellin into the hut
an he's got the heel (no guff)
the heel shot right off
his shoe

so he spends the next couple hours
sittin on his bunk   bummin smokes
an mutterin "Holy Shit"
over an over again

like I said
durin Jerry bombin raids
we'd hit for the trees
when actually we were supposed
to man these machine gun nests
spotted around the base

well
they were fun to practise on
but you see   every fourth shell
on those things was a tracer
so's you could supposedly zero in
on a target   but all's they did
was make it easier for Jerry
to see where we were

I'll tell you
I wasn't gonna tangle with no
Jerry fighter pilot
who could knock the balls
off a gopher from 500 yards

this new guy comes on base
an durin a raid jumps into
one of these anti-aircraft nests
gets lucky   an brings down
this Junkers 88 bomber
(an boy we kicked his arse
for that one!)

so anyways
the C.O. he figgers
we gotta give these dead krauts
full military honors   with a service
in the chapel   an honor guard
an no shit   someone even found a Jerry flag
to drape over one coffin

after that
they were just buried in a field
but after the war   I guess
they were dug up
an sent back to the Fatherland

nights were for thinkin
listenin   thinkin
about home   family
what the future might be

listenin
for the sound of kites
figgerin out whether they
were ours or maybe theirs

an after a while
it was easy to tell

ours sort of hummed
an easy sleepy moan

an theirs   Christ
theirs would pulse
would throb   an you'd
start sweatin   like
the Devil himself
was overhead
comin for your soul

so this one time
I put in to go to Africa
never got it   but I notice
all they ever sent there
was shit disturbers   like
bad buggers they could never
get a day's work out of

then after D day
they sent more of these guys
to the continent   where
there was nothin else
to do but work

see
you could tell a lot
about a guy just by askin
what bases he'd been on
like   the more transfers
the worse he probably was

an if he said   yeah   he'd been
to Dalton   well that was pretty much
the clincher right there
cause Dalton   holy shit
that was the worst   see
they'd mostly just load these guys
on lorries   drive them
ten miles into the moors
an drop them   to see
if they'd get back by supper

hell
wouldn't surprise me
if they never set eyes
on some of them
again   just swallowed up
or what the hell   maybe
still warmin some bird's sheets

R - Robert

well
it was no picnic either
cause it took fifteen to twenty men
to keep a kite in the air

see
on every dispersal
you had three kites   right
an runnin the show was
a sergeant an three corporals

us ground crew was usually
one mechanic for every engine
a couple air framers
for patch-ups on shell holes
shit like that   maybe
an electrician   an whatever joe boys
you could get assigned to you

air crew was the bomb aimer
who also manned the front gun on Lancs
then the pilot an flight engineer
in the cockpit   an behind them
the wireless operator an then
the navigator

back in the body
you had maybe a mid-upper gunner
an a tail gunner in the rear

U - Utopia

every squadron had twenty-six kites
divided into A an B flights
the first named from A to M
like A-Annie or B-Big Cat
an so on

ours was always E-Eden
an even when our kite went down
the next one was the same

an some hotshot artist
in the squadron would paint
a picture on the kite's nose
of a woman or an animal
some even had scripture

ours was a hula girl
an for every mission
over enemy territory we got
a little palm tree painted beside her

I recall one time
we got as high as twenty-six
palm trees   before she went down
maybe doesn't sound like much
but she was a record
for '43

in training
we'd do overhauls lots of times
in Canada   but once we got
overseas   one little snafu
an we pulled the whole engine
like nobody's business

like
sometimes you'd get a kite
that'd just been in a chase
some 109s flyin up their arse
poppin two-inch shells
around their ears

so the crew
wasn't too worried
about the engines   just
opened em up an hightailed it
home

you might not believe it
but swear to God
I worked on one kite
had four seized-up props

I can still see those guys
at full throttle   prayin
for the first time
since Sunday School

let's see
a kite would last you
around twenty-five missions   thirty
I heard once over in Swordfish squadron

old E-Eden musta went through
fifteen   twenty kites
an far as I know   an
we were luckier than most

even then
we didn't get too buddy-buddy
with many of our air crew   cause
while us ground crew
was there for the duration
air crew signed on
for only thirty missions
ya thirty   an then
they'd be rested

sure
a lot of them re-signed
for another tour   cause
the second choice was teachin
at flight school back in Canada

but
give em credit
survivin twenty-five was somethin
when you consider Bomber Command
musta been losin more'n
250 kites a month
in '43 an '44

you know
I still figger
we were pretty lucky
the way the krauts
ran their war

like
there were times
I figgered we'd have
to run for the hills
but Hitler managed
to screw up
somehow

you know?
take in '41
when he goes against Russia
so they have to divert
most of their bombers
over there

shit
it was still no picnic
for us   but I know
I got better shut-eye
once the buggers
went to Russia

we're always havin trouble
with the mid-upper gunner's turret
cause this valve would leak
an have to be replaced
every ten hours or so

well
back home
I'd always been a whiz
with Dad's tools   like
he'd show me some busted
tractor part   an I'd
grind one out
in no time

so me an this corporal
go at this valve one night
when we're waitin
for our kites
out on a raid

an damned
if we don't come up
with a valve that lasts
a hundred hours or more

well
one of the officers
gets wind of this   an takes it
down to London
to show the big shots

well
you coulda guessed it
this asshole comes back
with another ring around his sleeve
the corporal gets a three-day pass
an me   I get a mention
in dispatches   big deal

after that
I spent my nights
makin toys an jewellery
for my family on those lathes
piss on them   let somebody else
win their fuckin war

not too many times
in this whole mess
did I ever lose it
but one time
I came close

this Sunday afternoon
summer of '43   I think
we're lyin around our dispersal
relaxin   watchin the sky   so clear
like combining a hundred-mile swath

an these Harvard trainers
are showin off above us
just kids from flight school
havin a lark

but Lord sonny Jesus
if these 109s don't show up
cocky as hell   cause they
musta known the nearest Spitfires
are a half hour away

so they just circle those kids
like hawks watchin some field mice

of course
the Harvards don't wanna land
but they start runnin low
on fuel   so one by one
they try to come in
an the goddamn 109s just take turns
followin them in
cuttin them to shreds

six of them caught it
that way   an the rest
crash-landed in the woods
around the base

well
ten good kids never
got into that war
an besides   a couple
of those krauts probably
got their "ace"
for that day's work

on our base
we were always gettin
what we called "visiting aircraft"
which was a nice way
of sayin "shot all to hell
an can't get home"

this one Yankee kite comes in
an we count over two hundred holes
in the fuselage   plus
the flight engineer an bomb aimer
have bought it

the mid-upper gunner's
got some holes in him too
but he's still breathin
an screamin like a wounded rabbit
so they fill him full
of morphine before we can
winch him out

well
we're cleanin up
when one of the guys yells
from the rear   an when we go
back there we realize
this type of kite
has a tail gunner

sure enough
all that's left
is a hole so neat
a welder woulda been
proud of it

ana couple quarts
of his blood
splashed around the edge

we got a lot
of that "loose lips
sink ships" kind of stuff
an mostly laughed it off

but
I guess it
was serious enough
cause Lord Ha Ha gave
High Command a good scare
once in a while

like once he broadcasted
to our base an told us
exactly where our mission
was goin that night
not that us erks ever knew
but somebody musta bragged
to some bird in the pubs   shit
the whole of Bomber Group Six was C.B.ed
two weeks for that one

but like I said
he was mostly just a joke
an us Canucks were one
of his favorite targets
like the time he said
we had four divisions   two
in Canada   fightin
to get overseas   an two
in Britain   fightin
to get home

or he'd claim
if us Canucks ever tried
a caper like Dieppe again
the kraut police would go out
an arrest them

you know
after the war
they hanged the bastard

served him right
I say

45

I'm standin
under the wing
of a Halifax   talkin
to a mechanic
on the number four engine

when in comes
this kite   a Lanc I think
back from a raid   on fire
streamin that oily smoke
that's sinkin faster than
the Lanc even

well
it's carryin a full load
cause the bomb bay doors
musta jammed

he tries to make a landin
but his right gear collapses
an he disintegrates
scatterin debris an bombs
all over the tarmac

I head for some bush
a couple hundred yards away
the mechanic   he goes off the end
of the wing   hits the runway
an we both dive into the bush
about the same time

when the show settles down
I crawl over to him
an he's lien there
with two broken ankles
havin a smoke

things kinda got borin
for us erks   an once
in a while a guy
could wangle a ride
in a kite on a night mission

well
that stopped pretty quick
after one of our guys goes A.W.O.L.
for a couple months
till the krauts report him
as a P.O.W.

I'm glad
I wasn't the poor bugger
who had to explain
that one

I think
this company in Canada
was called Victory Aircraft
or somethin   an they built
a buncha Lancasters

course
most of them were assigned
to Number Six Bomber Group
an we were happy
cause that meant the tool kits
would be made in Canada too

see
you probably wouldn't know
but British tools they're the shits   nothin
but clumsy spanners
an screwdrivers that slip
every second turn

only problem is
the Lancs landed
on a British base first
an the R.A.F. get hold
of the kits and exchanged them
for theirs

an I know
you're tired of hearin
the same old tune
but guess who's
stuck with the shit

lotsa times
I'd volunteer to wait
in the shops for our kites
so's I could use
the machines   an stay out
of the officers' way

an when the raids left
it was the one time
I can say I really enjoyed
somethin about the war

see
they usually left
just before supper   one
every three or four minutes
till all twenty-six in our flight
were gone   an the sound
of the engines   engines
I'd worked on   gave me some pride
that I was doin somethin useful
other than pissin off
the brass

you could hear their hummin
for fifteen   twenty minutes
as they formed up   an headed
across the Channel

an then
durin that long silence
after   I'd fiddle around
on the lathes   makin these trinkets
I showed you   for the folks
back home

an anywhere between eleven
an daylight   back they'd come
not orderly this time
but in bits an pieces

you'd go out an start countin
prayin you'd get
to twenty or so   an knowin
anything after that
was a bonus

49

serviceability
now that was a word
we heard time an again over there
cause it was based on
what percentage of your kites
you could get in the air
every day

so our squadron
was always 100%
or damn close   an we didn't
know it   but no one else
came close

so all these big shots
would show up   half a dozen rings
around their sleeves   gold braid
up their arses   sometimes
a couple knock-out Wrens
slinkin along with them

(I'll tell you
once I was as close
as you to me
to Billy Bishop)

an you know
what they saw   more often
than not   was guys
out enjoyin the sun
playin ball   or just
relaxin in the huts

cause the secret for us
was simple   cooperation
just guys workin together
no one thinkin he was too good
for some little joe job
maybe doin another guy's
engine if he was on
a long leave   stuff like that

twenty-six kites   that's what
they asked   an sure as
Hitler had a dose
we'd have twenty-six
in the air   hummin along
with another load for the goddamn Fatherland

Yankees
let me tell you
about Yankees

see
they had their Flyin Fortresses
just limos packed full
of anti-aircraft guns
an luxuries for the crew
but what the hell
they were dumb enough
to go on daylight raids
so they may's well
go out in style

only problem was
they couldn't carry
more'n 20 000 pounds
of bombs

but the Lancaster boy
there was a delivery truck
no heating or pressure
control in the cockpit   an eventually
we tore off most of the guns
so's she could carry more
cause truth be known
a guy shootin at a fighter
with those guns
made about as much sense
as you an I throwin rocks
at a magpie

so the Lanc she ended up
deliverin more'n 30 000 pounds
to the Reich

like we used to say
not much to look at
but boy what a bugger to go

I guess
most people figger
a bomb goes off when it hits
the ground   but no way

you see
on the arse end of it
there's this propeller
an when the bomb is droppin
the prop   which is attached
to this threaded shaft
screws itself into a detonator
until the whole business blows

so the armourers   the guys
who load the bombs   have to set
the prop so's they'd blow
just a bit above ground
where they'd do the most damage

one other thing—
the threads were usually right-
handed   but once in a while
some left-hand
so's maybe a few krauts
on the bomb-defusing squads
would get blown up   or at least
have to sweat a bit
before finishin the job

this one day
I'm working late
on the number one engine
cause one of the other mechanics
he's on a three-day pass

an the bomb dollies
are pullin in underneath
loadin up for another raid

I just happen to look down
an damned if I don't see
one of the bomb props spinnin
slowly spinnin in the wind

I don't know
whether to shit or go blind
so I start screamin
at the armourers   an
one of them stops it
but we don't know
how many turns it's got to go
before the whole place goes up

so they call bomb disposal
an sweat for half an hour
cause I'm not leavin the engine
with the raid so close

they arrive
take the bomb an drop it in a pit
half a mile away
an a couple minutes later
it barks

so we go back to work
wonderin how we're gonna
get lucky next time

I'm readin the paper the other day
an I gotta chuckle   cause I see
this article sayin
Wing Commander so-an-so, D.F.M.
is promoted to Group Captain

what you don't know is
this guy   we called him Woody
was at our base   ana royal
pain in the royal Canadian

one day
this Lancaster limps in
all shot up   landin gear
jammed on one side
ana full bomb load
of course

it pranges all over the tarmac
an the erks are out there
helpin pull the crew loose
an rollin some of the bombs
outa the way

Woody is standin
about fifty yards away
yellin orders no one can hear
from behind this bomb dolly

an sure enough
a 250-pounder barks
killin two of our guys
an throwin a fragment
that rips off Woody's left hand

well
you can guess
what happened   ya
two letters from the padre
ana D.F.M. for Woody

55

Bombing up Halifax III

the armourers are winchin up
the bomb loads this one day
an they say they got somethin
a little extra for the Reich

you wouldn't know the difference but
it's a bomb
that doesn't go off right away
just delays an hour or so

seems Bomber Command figgers
we may's well blow up
a few kraut fire departments
while we're at it

this other time
we're out on the dispersal
an this Wimpy comes in
shot to shit   lookin like
it's gonna land
right on top of us

well
we take off in ten directions
an of course I'm the one
who guesses wrong   cause
I hear his tires hit
a couple hundred yards
behind me

then his brakes scream
an I guess they catch
on only one side   cause
when I look back   his wing tip
is swingin around   about
to shorten me a couple feet

well
the only thing
between me ana wheelchair
is these prop kits
piled up by the runway

I'm over them
an I hear the wing tip
zingin behind my head
while I'm still in the air

when the smoke clears
the guys figger I should
go to the Olympics   cause
those kits are piled
damn near six feet high

One of our gifts to Hitler—Christmas 1943

I remember
this one Christmas
we all get to paint the names
of our hometowns on this Tallboy
an then somethin like "Merry Xmas
to Adolf an the Third Reich"

a Tallboy?   ya
that was a twelve-thousand pounder
pretty big   but after that
there was the Grand Slam   get this—
twenty-two thousand pounds
but only for U-boat pens
an railway tunnels   shit
the Lancaster was the only kite
that could handle one of those

but mostly we just loaded up
with what were called G.P.s—
like   General Purpose
or General Nuisance as we said

then sometimes there'd be
a fire raid   so they'd need
these five-hundred pound clusters
each with about a hundred or so
incendiaries packed inside
like they used to roast
Dresden an Hamburg

but me
I never thought too much
about where they were goin
an I didn't wanta know

I wasn't aimin them
just gettin them off the ground

you know
what it's like
to watch ducks tryin to
land on a slough that's froze
an they don't know it
like a curling game gone wild

well
that's what a wash-out
looked like   when a pilot
just sort of reached the point
where he couldn't hack it
anymore

we had lots of them
oh   they could get the kite
into the air alright
but landing was
a different matter

an I guess
the flak   or the Messerschmitts
maybe the noise   or a dream
about what was happenin below
just got to him

so when he saw that runway
he realized too late
that this one wasn't
gonna work   an he usually
belly-flopped the whole business

luckily
he was flyin on fumes
by now   there weren't
many fires   an I guess
if any humour came outa
droppin tons of bombs on people
these wash-outs were
about as close
as we got

sometimes
just for hellery
you'd take a walk
down the runway
an maybe you'd come across
these sort of jacks
these ten-pointed items
sharp as tacks
that'd rip a good
two-inch hole
in a kite's tire

where they came from
I'm not sure   maybe dropped
from Jerry kites   or spies
(we always had lots
of stories about spies)
maybe spies threw
a handful   passin by

but it didn't matter   cause
just one of those
could sometimes save
the Fatherland from
ten tons of bombs

if I'da had my druthers
I'druther the Yanks had stayed home

we used to say
the buggers were over-paid
over-sexed   an over here

you shoulda seen em
in a raid   they had more ammo
than medals   an they'd
just go nuts   boy they could
make a hell of a noise
even if they could hit
bugger all

an they'd go out
on these daylight raids
with only one navigator
for a whole squadron
so if his kite got hit she was
game over   the rest
of them were suckin slough water
cause they had to find
their own way home

or worse yet
if they got socked in
at their base   maybe they'd land
at ours   not one by one
like our kites   but all at once
like a flock of spooked swallows
an Lord help us
if one went out of control

I guess the fact
they had lots of kites
an bombs sort of helped
get the war over earlier
but for my money
if they'da stayed home
an let us finish the job
I'da enjoyed my stay
a helluva lot more

if for some reason
our kites missed the target
or for some other reason
didn't get rid of their payload
they'd just dump the whole shitteree
in the Channel
on the way home

not so for the krauts

see
they'd always find
some British island or somethin
to unload on

so one time
we had this guy transfer in
from the Shetlands   an he said
they'd get it from Jerry
goin over   and comin back

so what did they do?
they just rigged up some lights
on the hills a couple miles away
an could sit back an enjoy the show
as those krauts blew the hell
outa that phony runway

sometimes
I wonder who got more
of our boys   the krauts
or our own stupidity

but
when you're sendin up
hundreds of kites every night
it's hard enough for them
to get back from the continent
let alone dodge our own
nightfighters

so this one night
one of our Lancs it gets shot down
by our own anti-aircraft yet

there's shit to pay
because the kites got
the wrong color lights on
an who's on the carpet
but this buddy of mine
another farm boy who's in supply

well
he gets his ass
out of the wringer toot sweet
cause he's got the requisitions
all signed good an proper

it turns out
some poor bugger   an air framer
on the dispersals
gets a quick trip to Africa
for that screw-up

we sure knew somethin was up
on D day   we sent up
our kites four times   the sky
was black with bombers

an I guess the army
was directin some of them
onto kraut targets
by ground radio

one of our crews
comes back lookin
kinda sick

seems
they get orders
to drop their load
right after this water tower

only problem
was there was two towers
one on the kraut side
of the line   an one on ours

well
you can guess
which one they saw first

I don't think
Bomber Command started thinkin
till about '44

well look
up till then Ole "Bomber" Harris
the C.O. of Air Force C.O.s
figgered the way to beat the krauts
was to bomb hell
outa their cities an demoralize them

well
the dumb bugger coulda
looked around London   an seen
that people just get pissed off
more'n scared

then
we dropped thousands of tons
on their sub pens   a complete
piss into the wind
cause we couldn't dent
twenty yards of concrete
till the Grand Slam was built

but in '44 we started
goin after their railways
an fuel supplies

after that
Jerry couldn't move like he wanted
like   couldn't get his fighters
in the air   or maybe his Panzers
from one place to the next
which was one reason
D day went so well for us

hell
I read up on this
an in '44 an '45
Number Six Bomber Group
had the lowest casualties
in the whole Command
just because some guys
with gold rings on their sleeves finally
started thinkin a bit

who sez
there wasn't some good things
come outa the war   hell

lots of times
when things got rough
someone would come up
with the answer

like
would you believe
the first couple years
they were usin carrier pigeons
to send messages back
from kites

as far as bombin accuracy
when it got obvious
daylight raids were suicide
we started usin stars an landmarks
to guide out kites   hell
it was a miracle
if any damage was done
ana true act of God
if they got back
to the right base

then when the first crude radar
was invented   we used what was called
the Cat an Mouse system   the Cat
bein the radar station
that guided our kites along this arc
that the target was on   an the Mouse
bein another station that zeroed in
on the actual target

but then
the krauts got better radar
an shot hell out of us again

so we used
what we called "window"
these strips of tin foil
that drove their screens nuts

an what did Jerry do?
invented better radar
an shot our arses off again

so we got these jammers
we sent ahead of our kites
in Mosquitoes   an that confused them
again for a while

pretty soon
we had this H2S system
where you could bounce signals
offa bridges an rivers

an by the end
who knows   we were probably
gettin within a couple hundred
yards of the target

there were hundreds of women
in Leeds   workin
in the small arms plants
so that's where we headed
on our short leaves

we'd get all spiffed up
but no luggage   no
just some soap   a wash cloth
ana few condoms in the lining
of our dress blues

before we could leave though
they'd herd us in
for short arm inspection
an maybe the M.O.
'd show us a film

boy
we'd all be sweatin
lookin at these flicks
of some poor bugger
with his privates rotted
damn near off

then the M.O.
he'd say he heard
there was a virgin in Leeds
an she'd just been born
that morning

or he'd tell us
there was one sure way
of avoidin a dose
so we'd be all ears
an he'd yell   "Stay home!"

anyways
there were times
we left the base with mixed feelings
about whether we should
concentrate on drinkin
or the birds

you needed a pound a day
for a three-day leave   that is
if you wanted a little social life

but
you only got
a pound ana half
at pay parade   so you hadda
double your money somehow

well
craps was one way
an sometimes it worked   but
sometimes you'd crap out
the first couple throws

then the only thing to do
was quit smokin
for a couple weeks
an sell your fags to some Pongo
for a few shillings

but then
it was damn hard
to impress the birds
with shillings   so it
usually ended up with
a shilling to sleep
at the Salvation Army
a shilling for breakfast
a quick tour of the sights
ana few beers in the pubs

now
I don't want you
to think I'm sayin
all English women were tarts

oh sure
morals were a bit looser
I guess   what with people
not knowin what the future held

but more often than not
you'd just buy a girl a drink
have a few dances so's
she could size you up
an maybe she'd ask you
if you wanted to see
her place

an there'd be
her Mom an Dad   they might give
you a bit of lunch
I remember one time
all they had was these
pickled onions an bread
no butter of course
cause there was none to be had

they seemed quite interested
in Canada   any little fact
that proved we weren't all
just fishermen or loggers
would amaze them

an I gotta say
I enjoyed just sittin there
bein with a family
again

I think on the whole
the Brits liked us Canucks
a bit more than the Yanks
an no matter what some guys
might tell you   that's how
most of our dates ended up

we had to go down
to this base in Glouster once
to work on some new Lancasters
that'd just arrived from Canada

so one weekend
we went into the city
just to look around   an hell
it was great   the people
stopped us on the streets
to ask who we were
an some even bought us
a drink

but we caught on
to what was happening
pretty quick   when we
realized that this city
was full of Yanks   an we
were a novelty for these Brits
who'd tell us to take
the Yanks with us
when we went back
to York

fat chance of that
cause we knew they'd get
the same treatment as us
back in York   where the Brits
were most likely tired
of seein us Canucks

it seemed like
some nights   if we met
up with some Yanks
it was guaran-ass-teed
there'd be a fist fight

funny thing
we didn't even get along
with the Pongos so well
until the Yanks showed up

then there were times
we'd have a run-in
with the Free French
but they weren't up to much
an the Norwegians couldn't fight
worth shit neither

but I'll tell you
one place we stayed clear of
was Glasgow   cause no matter
how tough you thought you were
that's where the Poles were
an they were undisputed champs

Christ
they were mean   like
four against one was about
a fair fight

I don't know
what got them so pissed off
but maybe all they had
to think about was gettin home
an havin to choose between
the Nazis and the Reds

so we won a few
an lost a few against the others
but the Poles   I'll tell ya
undi-frickin-sputed champs

somethin
I forgot to tell ya
was one time I'm in London
on a weekend pass   an damned
if I don't come across
this guy from home
attached to army transport

well
he's tight as a lord
cryin in his beers
an he tells me his unit
just transported the Princess Pats
down to the docks a couple days ago

well they find out
the Pats just hit the beaches
at Dieppe

that morning
they go down to pick them up
and how many do you figger
he collects

you guessed it
zero   shit squared
not one

one time
I get hold of Ronnie Clark
whose Dad farmed a mile
down the road from us

we meet in York
an damned if we don't see
this fella across the street
who was a couple years
behind us in school

we run over
pat him on the back
an say   "Hey Bobby
long time no see!"

well I guess we missed
some braid or somethin
cause you know what he says?
get this "Don't you erks
know enough to salute
an officer?"

well
right away me an Ronnie
plan this get-together
at this pub in York
send out invites
to a couple dozen guys from home
we know are in the area

it's quite a deal—
eighteen show up   includin Bobby
an we really put on
the feed bag

when we're done
we sit around B.S.in
an most of us know what's up

so
one guy has to go to the john an
one guy has to use the phone
one has to buy some smokes
one has to thank the cook
an so on   till all that's left
is Ronnie me an Bobby

Bobby doesn't catch on
till the owner sets the bill
on the table in front of him

when he looks up
there's me an Ronnie
with our wedges on
salutin an sayin
"Up yours, sir!"
as we hightail it
out the door

once
when I got a week's leave
I figgered I'd better see
some of the sights in London
before we were shipped home

so I got billeted
with this family   nice folks
an I was sleepin upstairs
when the house starts to shake

their boy yells up
that some buzz bombs are comin in
an I should come outside
to their bomb shelter

well
all it is
is this hole in the yard
with some corrugated tin
over top   so I said
I'd take my chances inside

after an hour or so
an seven barks   I wander
out to see the damage

well
the closest they got to us
was this park nearby
where the Brits had planted
what they called
one of their Victory Gardens
mostly cabbage an carrots
for the war effort

the crater
was right in the middle
about a yard deep
an ten feet across

an it'd blown every leaf
off the trees   but replaced them
with a nice new coat
of shredded cabbage

she was a WAC
I met in London
down a bomb shelter

she held onto my arm
so tight   her nail marks
were there a week later

after the "all clear"
she asked if I'd get a room
an stay with her
cause she couldn't stop
shakin

in the morning
we got talkin   an damned
if she wasn't raised
about thirty miles
south of our place

funny
I never saw her again
never looked for her either

this one night
this young guy's on guard duty
but he's tryin to trade
with one of us
so's he can keep a date
in Leeds   he says is a sure thing

well
this kid's got
a reputation for not carin
if the cow calves
or busts her ass tryin
so no one's willin to help him out

but
I'm goin in anyways   so
I say I'll make the big sacrifice
an meet her so's the date
can be rescheduled

an hour later
here I am   lookin for this corner
where she's supposed to be
waitin   an it's dark
as a coal bin

I wait for a half hour
an I'm about to give up
when I hear footsteps

as they get closer
I can make her out
an the sure thing doesn't
look much better than
some mud fences I seen

anyways
it turns out
this is her mother
comin to tell our guy
the girl couldn't make it

didn't matter anyhow
we found out a week later
some guy from Thunderbird Squadron
got the clap from her

I remember
walking the streets
of Manchester this one time
a little drunk   or as drunk
as you could get
on that horse piss
they called beer

so I'm tryin
to nose out a chip shop
bangin into light posts
that haven't lit up in years

an all at once   there she was
in the half-dark   like a vision
in her doorway   fur coat
(not a real one   of course)
hair to her shoulders
an made up real nice

she whips open the coat
to show her wares
all garters an lace
sayin "Half a crown, luv?"
(it was always half a crown)
but I just stand there
starin a few seconds
till she sort of pouts
an slams the door

well
it wasn't the first
or last time it happened
to me   but
the only thing I remember
thinkin at the time was
she was probably
somebody's mother

an over the years
every time I think of her
she seems to have got
more beautiful   till
I sometimes wonder
what difference
that half a crown
woulda made in my life

Ronnie an me
kept pretty close touch
through the whole thing cause
we were both about a half hour
from York   so we'd meet
for supper once in a while

this one time
we got carried away
so it was pretty dark

there was always trucks
goin back to the bases
before midnight   an Ronnie
caught one for his   but mine
musta taken off already

well
a blackout is like it says
an if there's no moon
it's like bein struck blind

once you were outa town
you'd just stand there squintin
an like Ronnie would say
dark as the inside of a cow

but once you made out
the horizon   you'd just make
a bee line for home

so there I was
bumpin into hedges an stone fences
an once
to get a better view
I stood on this rock
that turned out to be a cow
scared the shit outa both of us

well
I was about to give up
when damned if our kites
didn't show up
back from a raid

God
it was the first time
I was glad to see a Lancaster

an I just looked up
runnin after their lights
like a crazy man
as they drifted into base

you shoulda seen them

they get here
after the worst is over
an move in
like they own the place

Fuckin Yanks
you'd go for a beer
an they'd be movin in
on all those Brit maidens
showin off their medals for K.P.
money and smokes just fallin
outa their arseholes

this one night
at the Crown & Cushion
I'm pretty tight an fed up
so I start for base on my bike
when I see Andy   tight
as a bull fighter's pants
facin down this crowd of Yanks
he figgered were musclin in
on his action

I could see no good
was gonna come outa this
so I just ran my bike
between him an the biggest Yank
sayin somethin intelligent
like   "Time for home, Andy!"

I guess
the Yanks were so shocked
they didn't know
whether to swing or sway

well
Andy's a salesman now
an you can bet once a year
sure as hell   he'll show up here
wantin to buy me a beer
an thankin me again
for the time I saved his life

we're havin a pretty good time
in this pub one night
but it's kinda tense
cause quite a number of these
American Guardsmen are there too

I don't know
if I said somethin
or looked the wrong way
at this Yank   but he comes over
puffed up like a nickle balloon
an tells me we're goin outside
to have it out

he's a big bugger
but I follow him out
anyways   ana ring forms up
in the street

I'm waitin for the worst
when this buddy   Hank Watson
steps in an sez
"Hey Yank   I'm more your size
Why not try me?"

the Yank doesn't care
so he tells Hank
to take the first shot

"Nope!" Hank sez
as he puts his hands in his pockets
"You're the guy lookin
for the fight! You go ahead!"

well
the Yank starts throwin
haymakers   an Hank   real cool
just side-steps them
with that dumb smile of his

finally
the Yank just puts his hands
behind his back an yells
"OK! Come on! Hit me!
Come on, you bastard!"

85

so I step
into the ring an let him have it
right in the family jewels

Jesus
even the Yanks crack up
an we're all laughin so hard
we're outa there
before they can figger out
whether to shit or go blind

you know
at the end
when the Luftwaffe was scuttled
an all they had left
was the buzz bombs
we were doin these
low level daylight raids

after one of these
this bomb aimer comes off
his kite   with a real funny look
on his face

they hadn't even been scratched
so I ask him what's up

an he says
he's lookin through his sights
right over the target
an God damned if he doesn't see
these people on the ground
lookin straight up at him

I guess his finger froze
on the release switch
an that cargo was left
in the Channel
on the way home

Electrical Section, RCAF Station, Eastmoor, Yorkshire, June 1944

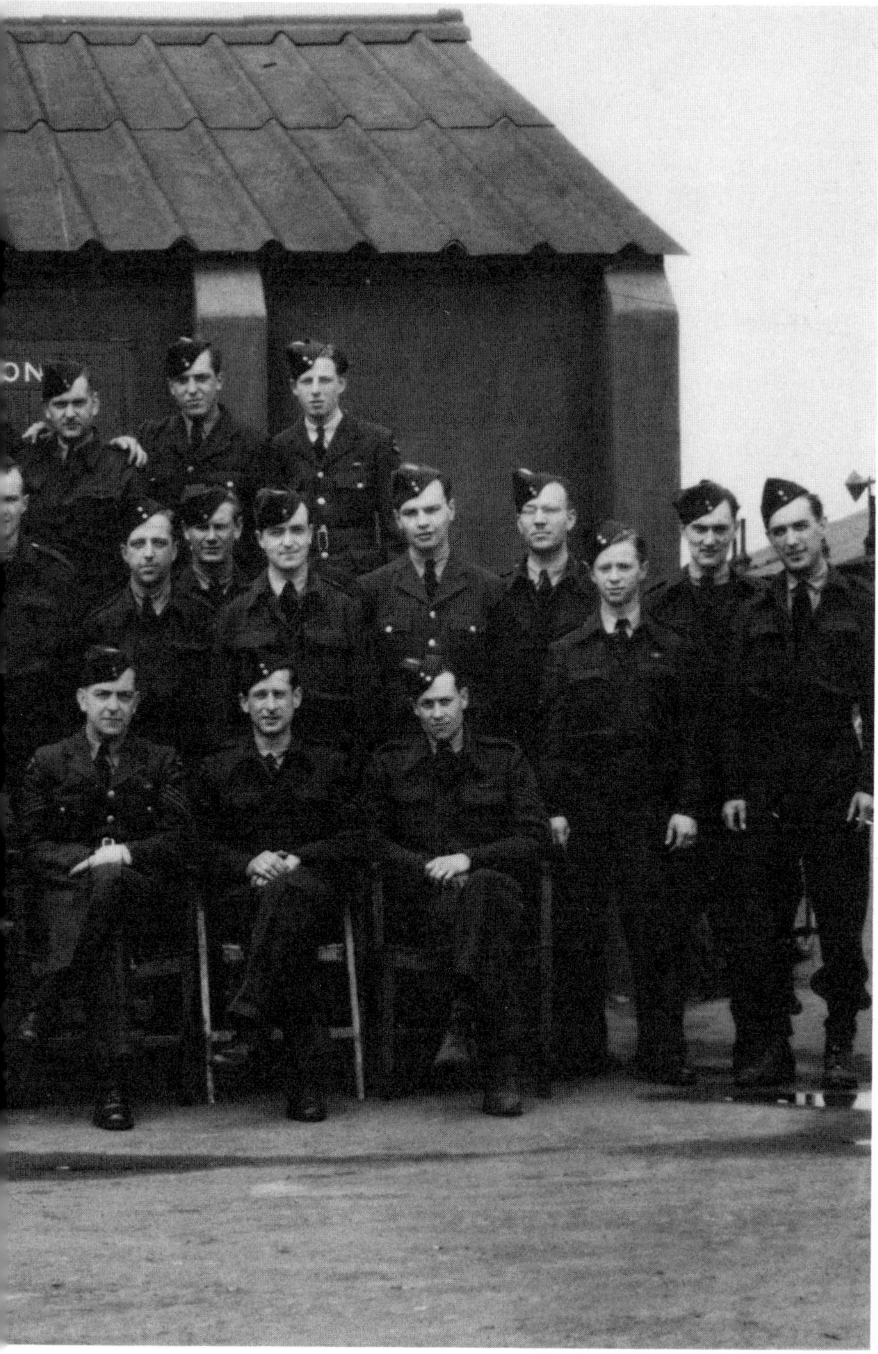

towards the end
when we had the air
pretty much to ourselves
we'd go out to the coast
on a weekend pass
an watch these stripped-down Spitfires
chase down buzz bombs
as they came across the Channel

I guess
earlier they'd shot at them
but the blasts took
a couple of Spits with them
plus some people on the ground
who couldn't dodge the debris

so this way
they'd just fly
up beside the doodlebugs
touch the rudders
with their wing tips
an send them off course
into the drink

then
when we got jets
all's they had to do
was fly in front of them
an put them off balance
with their slip streams

that is
until the V-2 came along
an shit boys
there wasn't a thing
we could do   except
kick the Reich's arse
a little harder with our raids

V-E Day
boy   I got a story
to tell you about that

you see
the bells started ringin
in the morning   an when
we heard the news
the whole base cleared
into the towns

a few beers later
I get this crazy idea
I'm gonna go see these cousins
my Mom had been writin me
an buggin me to visit
all through the war

it's only a few miles away
an when I arrive about tea time
they hadn't heard the news
about the krauts capitulatin
an they're so happy about that
an seein me   they take off
into town to buy some booze
an food   so's we can throw
this party to end all parties

sure enough
the next time I see them
is about noon the next day
an they don't even thank me
for mindin their livestock

I'll tell you
on V-J Day this cat
just stuck to the pubs

talk about chicken one day
an feathers the next

word came through
pretty soon after V-E Day
they were flyin our kites
directly back to Canada
an the air crew sez
they're takin us erks with them

hell
we've got our duffle bags packed
out on the dispersals
an we're loadin the wheel jacks
an tool kits   when the news comes
the big shots have decided
the commissioned ranks are goin
home first

boy
our air crews are pissed off
they even threatened not to go
but when they were told
they'd be left behind too
we told them to forget it

I guess
the thing that pissed me off
the most was some of the guys
who loaded up that day
had been in Britain
only a couple months
an here they were
getting the first-class ride
back home

an us erks
ya   we were left
scratchin our arseholes
as usual

a couple weeks later
one of the guys
in the orderly room
tells us they got this letter
from High Command   sayin
they're givin our squadron
two D.F.M.'s, an A.F.C., ana D.F.C.
plus a pile of oak leaves
to distribute however we want

right away we start
thinkin about some of the raids
when men did enough for a V.C.
an even some of the erks
who'd bought it
savin guys from wrecks
or rollin live bombs outa fires

we shoulda guessed though

a week later
the same guy tells us
the C.O. sends this note over
sayin "Distribute the medals
as you see fit. I'll take
the D.F.C."

so it's obvious
we're the last ones
gonna get home   an they C.B.ed us
at Tempsford   a place not fit
for an outhouse rat

so here's 200 guys
the war's six months over
we're sleepin in crumblin huts
dead of winter   on moldy mattresses
eatin rotten food   an worst of all
only two packs of smokes a week

an the last straw
is when our officers get the boat home
an we're stuck with these Pongos
these Home Guard Brits
struttin around screamin orders
salutin   expectin the same from us
an generally makin life miserable

well
we took that for about two weeks
then one day just threw
our breakfast on the mess hall floor
piled our mattresses in the square
an sat there in our great coats
ignorin the Brits while they
jumped around like magpies
on a horse turd   threatening
firing squads an court martials

about mid-afternoon
up drives this big car   all flags
an out gets this Canuck Group Captain
who walks over an real calm
sez   "OK boys, what's it all about?"

we give him the lowdown
an before you know it
we got regular R.A.F. officers
carpenters fixin our huts
new mattresses   a decent meal
once in a while

an ya
a truckload of smokes

if you can believe it
a hell of a lot worse things
happened after V-E Day
than before

like
brawls   riots
murders even
when some Brit soldiers got home
an found their girlfriends
shacked up   or their wives
with a couple extra kids

an even guys who'd made it
fifty or sixty missions
might end up gettin killed
in a street fight
or barroom brawl

just over in Durham
one cocky Pongo officer
started in on some Canucks
so they stripped him
paddled his arse
an threw him offa bridge

only trouble was
the water was only
a foot deep   an the poor bugger
broke his neck

we even had a problem
one day in a cafe
when some Brit major
tells the waiter to ask us
to leave   we had to hold back
Andy till that s.o.b. left

so after a while
we got C.B.ed
an just sat around
playin cards an writin
letters home

I know exactly
where I was
at that moment—

changin guns on a Lancaster
bound for the Eastern front
an word came the Yanks
had flattened those cities
with their A-bombs

well
they can say what they want
but I can't remember
one guy blamin the Yanks
for doin it

we were just glad
it was all over

I guess
if I'da stayed in
I'd be pullin down
a nice pension by now

but when they finally
got us a boat
we just sat on our bunks
close to tears   most of us
not believin it was over

we talked
about what we'd do
once we got home   the wives
girlfriends   bosses
farms we were once glad
to escape

an we damn near fell over
when Gregoire an Belanger says
they're signin on
for another hitch

I guess
if we figgered
we had a depression out West
it wasn't half as bad
as the average day
in the backwoods of Quebec
where three squares a day
an free clothes didn't just
come walkin down the road
every day

oh
I don't think
I'da done it
any different though   but
at least I had a choice

I never really hated
the Germans   fact is
in a way
I sorta respected the buggers

I figger at the end
we just kinda outnumbered them
with men an material
or the thing coulda gone on
for another ten years or so

their fighter pilots
were somethin to behold
we lost a WAC once who forgot
to close a foot-square window
in her bunker durin a Jerry raid

this 109 pilot hardly
wasted a shell   blew her
damn near in half

but somebody
hadda teach them
you can't take on the whole world
an not expect a shit-kickin

the rooms on the Queen Mary
were meant for four
but for us
they had fifteen bunks
in each of them

forty-five to a room
fifteen in the bunks   fifteen
on the floor   fifteen
on deck   an we'd rotate
every night

durin the day
it got pretty rowdy on deck
with the craps games an all
so I just stuck to my bunk

this Flight Sergeant next to me
an old World War One vet
asks me to look after his kit
while he's topside
takin in the craps

an
every so often
down he comes
with his battle jacket
stuffed with two-dollar bills
which is what we got paid with
just before we left Britain

he opens up one of his bags
to stuff the dough in
an damned if it isn't
full to the top
with English pounds
an two-dollar bills

he looks at me
an sez "Boy   I fought
in the first one
an came home with nothin!
This time I'm takin somethin
back with me!"

the first few days out
some of the officers tried
to keep a bit of order
cause the decks were covered
with poker games an craps

but they smartened up
when most of the boys
just ignored them
or told them the war was over
an they could join in
or piss off

I guess
they finally saw that
some felt stripes on your arm
weren't as important as
gettin home in one piece

I was on the upper deck
one day   an noticed a ruckus
below me   an M.P.—some zombie
who'd spent his war in Halifax
was tellin one of our boys
near the depth charges
to put out his smoke

our boy tells him
to shove it   an where was he
when the bombs were droppin

the M.P. makes the mistake
of raisin his billy stick an
before you could blink
four of them grabbed him
an heaved him over the side

nobody said a word

they just threw him
a life raft an watched him
swim for it   as he
went out of sight

things settled down
after a while   an about
the only thing interesting
that went on was speculation
whether all the kraut U-boats
knew the war was over yet

an pretty soon
we musta gone south
cause we could suntan
all day long

then damned
if there weren't oranges
the odd chocolate bar
an stories that a couple
hundred war brides
were below decks

we hit the U.S. coast
off the Carolinas
then headed north
till we needed our great coats
again   but that was okay
cause it meant home
was near

we're a day out
of Halifax   an I can
just smell that home cookin
figgerin there's not much else
the Air Force can do to me

wrong again
cause this smell comes up
from the galley somewhere
like all the rotten mutton
we had to eat overseas
was bein shipped home with us

an it wasn't long
before we figgered it out—
the bastards are givin everybody
one last round
of short arm

they demobbed us
in Halifax   an I was happy
leavin all that blue
an bullshit behind

the last desk
before Civvie Street
was for our decorations
I got the E.B.G.O.   you know
Every Bugger Got One

but
just as I was leavin
the corporal sez
"Hey buddy
I see you were mentioned
in dispatches. That's worth
an oak leaf you know!"

"How much in cash?" I asks

"About sweet tweet" he sez

"What about
that carton of smokes?"

I still wonder
what line of bullshit
he tells his kids
about that oak leaf

there's one thing
I'da done different

look at me
got this bad back
high blood pressure
an I coulda been drawin
a burnt-out pension by now
if I'da got everything down
on paper

but
when I finally got around
to seein an M.O. in Halifax
he tells me my blood pressure
is up a bit   but the drinkin
probably did that   didn't it?
so he doesn't have to
mark it down   does he?
an my back
well I was so glad
to be goin home
I never even mentioned that

ten years later
when I'm off work
for the first time
I can't even remember
the M.O.'s name
so I'm screwed

shit
there's guys right in town
here   who're drawin
a damn good check every month
for some scar they probably got
fightin over some bird
an I'm sittin here
with Sweet Fanny Adams

you like pictures of horses?
just look at these beauties
cost me damn near nothin too

sure
after Paris was liberated
a guy could sneak a flight
on a supply plane
an take in the sights

well
the one thing they tell you
is to take lots of smokes
so I got my bag
stuffed with cartons

I see what they mean
cause on every street corner
you can find a Frenchman
sellin anythin you can imagine
an a couple you can't
for a few fags

this one
has these pictures of horses
an all he wants is five cartons
each   but I get him down
to three for both of them

jeez
one time my kid
comes home from college
with this girl who sez
some famous French painter
made them   an they should
be in a museum

piss on that noise
I tells her   they costed me
three cartons of fags

I guess
it's damn near all gone
by now   my kids used to ask me
why I didn't bring home
more stuff

boy
I remember those bins
where we threw our tin pots
bayonets   canteens   whatever
damned if I wanted
to drag it home

oh
I had my uniforms
for a while   but I wore out
the pants gardening   an the coats
finally went in the rag bag
after the kids dragged them
around playin war

but I got these stories
right?   ana lot of buddies
I still see
once in a while

otherwise
I don't think too much
about it all

it happened
I went
I got back   pretty well
in one piece

that's all

GLOSSARY

A.F.C.: *(Military)* Air Force Cross.

A.W.O.L.: *(Military)* Absent or absence without leave.

bird: *(British slang)* A girl or girlfriend.

Blenheim: An early twin-engine bomber.

brass: *(U.S. informal)* High-ranking military officers.

Canuck: *(Informal)* Any Canadian.

C.B.: Confined to base.

C.O.: Commanding officer.

D day: In military operations, the unspecified date of the launching of an attack; especially, June 6, 1944, the day on which the Allies invaded France in WW II.

demob: *(British informal)* To demobilize.

D.F.C.: *(Military)* Distinguished Flying Cross.

D.F.M.: *(Military)* Distinguished Flying Metal.

duster: *(U.S. slang)* A Western movie.

flak: Antiaircraft fire.

flicks: *(Slang)* Motion pictures.

Halifax: A bomber.

Jerry: *(Chiefly British slang)* A German; especially, a German soldier.

kite: *(British slang)* Any bomber.

K.P.: Kitchen patrol.

kraut: *(Slang)* A German; especially, a German soldier: an offensive term.

LAC: Leading aircraftsman.

Lanc: From Lancaster. A bomber.

lorry: *(British)* A truck.

Luftwaffe: *(German)* The German airforce during WW II.

Maggie's drawers: A reference to a bawdy pub song, "The Old Baggy Drawers that Maggie Wore."

Messerschmitt: 1898-1978, German aircraft designer and manufacturer. The 109 Messerschmitt was a fighter.

M.O.: Medical officer.

M.P.: Military police.

mucker: *(British slang)* A coarse, rude person; someone who does the most menial work in mines.

Pongo: *(Canadian slang)* British officer; a derogatory term.

P.O.W.: Prisoner of war.

prange: *(Slang)* A description of the wreckage of a crash-landed bomber.

R.A.F.: Royal Air Force (British).

R.C.A.F.: Royal Canadian Air Force.

short arm inspection: *(Slang)* The inspection of a military man's private parts to determine whether he has venereal disease.

skivvy: *(U.S. slang)* A man's underwear.

Sterling: A bomber.

Stuka: A German dive bomber.

U-boat: A German submarine.

V-E Day: May 8, the date of victory of the Allies in Europe in WW II, 1945.

V-J Day: September 2, the official date of the victory of the Allies over Japan in WW II, 1945.

WAC: A member of the Women's Army Corps.

Wimpy: *(Slang)* A Wellington, a type of bomber.

W.O.: Warrent officer.

Yank: *(Informal)* From Yankee. Any citizen of the United States.

STEPHEN SCRIVER

Stephen Scriver was born and raised in Wolseley, Saskatchewan. He attended the University of Saskatchewan in Saskatoon, graduating in 1969 with a B.A., and receiving a Diploma in Education the next year. Over the years, Scriver has had poems published in several Canadian journals: *Grain, CVII, Writing, NeWest Review, Event* and *This Magazine*. His poems have also appeared in the Coteau anthologies *Number One Northern* (1977), *100% Cracked Wheat* (1983) and *A Sudden Radiance* (1987), as well as in *The Maple Laugh Forever* and the school textbooks, *Contexts* and *Destinations*. Scriver has three previous books of poetry: *More! All Star Poet* (Coteau, 1989), *All Star Poet!* (Coteau, 1981) and *Between the Lines* (Thistledown, 1977).

Under the Wings is based on recollections of Scriver's father, Harry, and other "erks"—the aircraftsmen or groundcrew of World War II.

Scriver now teaches in Maidstone, Saskatchewan and commutes to his family in Edmonton where his wife, Barb, pursues her career as a midwife. He is currently working on a manuscript about the Medicare crisis in Saskatchewan in the 1960s.